Journal *to* Your Power

TRISH MOORE
Your Life Coach

ISBN 978-1-64299-670-8 (paperback)
ISBN 978-1-64299-671-5 (digital)

Copyright © 2019 by Trish Moore

All rights reserved. No part of this publication may be reproduced, distributed, or transmitted in any form or by any means, including photocopying, recording, or other electronic or mechanical methods without the prior written permission of the publisher. For permission requests, solicit the publisher via the address below.

Christian Faith Publishing, Inc.
832 Park Avenue
Meadville, PA 16335
www.christianfaithpublishing.com

Printed in the United States of America

This book is:
- Your hope
- Your empowerment
- Your self-help
- Your friendship
- Your faith
- Your courage
- Your love
- Your peace
- Your happiness

Your book to your power.

It will bring you power:
- Within yourself
- For yourself
- From yourself

Table of Contents

Introduction 7

Day one: feel 11
Day two: smile 15
Day three: help 19
Day four: learn 23
Day five: meditate 27
Day six: share 31
Day seven: read 35
Day eight: focus 39
Day nine: listen 43
Day ten: pray 47
Day eleven: reaching out 51
Day twelve: apologize 55
Day thirteen: compliment 59
Day fourteen: work on 63
Day fifteen: change 67
Day sixteen: begin 71
Day seventeen: hug 75
Day eighteen: redo 79
Day nineteen: commit 83
Day twenty: stop 87

Day twenty-one: encourage 91
Day twenty-two: improve 95
Day twenty-three: forgive 99
Day twenty-four: let go of 103
Day twenty-five: treat yourself 107
Day twenty-six: laugh about 111
Day twenty-seven: believe 115
Day twenty-eight: forget about 119
Day twenty-nine: stand up for 123
Day thirty: love 127

Conclusion 132

Introduction

I encourage you to journal daily, creating chapters of empowerment for you; by you. Journaling helps you think clearly and accomplish your most important task you have on your mind. It also helps you release inner thoughts you have inside.

Journaling is therapeutic and helps you prioritize, and conquer emotional and mental feelings of things you want to say to others. It helps you focus on goals and reduces stress.

Journaling empowers you to be the best "YOU" you can be.

Encouraged by: Me
Written by: You

JOURNAL TO YOUR POWER

Let's start today.

YOUR POWER

Let's journal our feelings.

Feel

To feel or feelings . . .

To be aware of or to experience an emotion or sensation. We can feel many ways: happy, sad, lonely, angry, or fulfilled. Many times we keep all these feelings locked up inside of us.

Did you know it's really not good to keep negative feelings locked up inside?

Emotionally, it causes hidden depression or even sickness. Journaling your feelings helps you open your thoughts and emotions. Whatever they are, express them.

Let's journal our feelings.

YOUR POWER

Day One – 1

Today I feel . . .

___
___
___
___
___
___
___
___
___
___
___
___
___
___
___
___
___
___
___
___
___
___

JOURNAL TO YOUR POWER

What, why, because . . .

YOUR POWER

ALWAYS

"share your smile with the world. It's a symbol of friendship and peace."
...Christie Brinkley

Smile

A smile can be a powerful thing; it's easy. It's non - judging, it's friendly, and it makes you feel good. You never know what someone can be feeling at any time. People don't always share when they are feeling sad, depressed, or angry.

Did you know that many people are walking around in need of a friendly *smile* and don't even know it? Giving a smile to anyone that is sickly can make them feel better instantly. Giving a smile to an elderly person makes them feel young again. Giving a smile to a toddler can make them feel safe.

Giving a smile to anyone at any time is always welcoming.

Don't forget to look in the mirror and smile for that person, you.

Let's give away smiles today, they're free.

YOUR POWER

Day Two – 2

Today I will smile about . . .

JOURNAL TO YOUR POWER

What, why, because . . .

YOUR POWER

YES

"Never look down on someone unless you're helping them up."
...Jesse James

Help

The definition of help is to make it easier for someone by offering one's services or resources. Giving of yourself just by listening is also an act of help. Most importantly, please don't ever be afraid to express the need for yourself if you need help in any way, shape, or form.

Open your mouth, your emotions, your eyes, and your heart and seek help.

Please ask for help, look for help, appreciate help, and accept help. Help is a blessing to give and receive. Where are you with the word help? Ready to give or ready to *receive*?

YOUR POWER

Day Three – 3

Today I will help . . .

___
___
___
___
___
___
___
___
___
___
___
___
___
___
___
___
___
___
___
___
___

JOURNAL TO YOUR POWER

Who, why, because . . .

YOUR POWER

GIFT

"develop a passion for learning. If you do, you will never cease to grow."
...by Anthony J D'Angelo

Learn

Learning is the knowledge or skills through experience, study, or being taught by someone.

Learning can be exciting, fun and challenging all at the same time.

Getting educated is priceless and can never be taken away. It's yours to keep.

You can also learn from your mistakes to help you move on to something better.

Learning is one of the keys to *success*, and that's no secret.

YOUR POWER

Day Four – 4

Today I will learn . . .

JOURNAL TO YOUR POWER

What, why, because . . .

YOUR POWER

EMBRACE

"the thing about meditation is you become more and more you."
...David Lynch

Meditate

To think deeply or focus one's mind for a period of time in silence or with the aid of chanting for religious or spiritual purposes or as a method of relaxation.

Meditation clears your mind, body, and spirit. It relaxes you from the inside out. Meditation makes you feel weightless and worry-free. The more you meditate, the better you can think and understand what's going on in your head, and what's going on around you. Meditating and sitting still with relaxing music not only relaxes your mind but also relaxes your body.

Meditation is a silent, unspoken word that we forget about but is needed.

YOUR POWER

Day Five – 5

Today I will meditate on . . .

JOURNAL TO YOUR POWER

What, why, because . . .

YOUR POWER

WE

"the miracle is: the more we share the more we learn."
...Leonard Nimoy

Share

Sharing is to have a portion of something with others; to split or divide or give half of.

Sharing our feelings and thoughts also bring people closer together.

A sharing person is generous and willing to give.

Sharing is humbling, helpful, and unselfish.

Sharing can make you feel warm and fuzzy inside.

Sharing is caring.

YOUR POWER

Day Six – 6

Today I will share my feelings with . . .

_____
_____
_____
_____
_____
_____
_____
_____
_____
_____
_____
_____
_____
_____
_____
_____
_____
_____
_____
_____
_____

JOURNAL TO YOUR POWER

Who, why, because . . .

YOUR POWER

ALOT

"reading is to the mind what exercise is to the body"
...Joseph Addison

Read

To look at and comprehend written material. It is the ability to understand words and symbols composed together.

Reading can take you to a different world mentally.

Read a book.
Read the newspaper.
Read a magazine.
Read a poem.
Read the Bible.

Reading is knowledge.
Reading is powerful.
Reading is entertaining.
Read, Read, Read . . .

YOUR POWER

Day Seven – 7

Today I will read . . .

JOURNAL TO YOUR POWER

What, why, because . . .

YOUR POWER

ME

*"stay focused go after your dreams
and keep moving toward your goals"
...LL Cool J*

Focus

Ability to pay attention to something without being distracted. Ability to look at with great interest and belief. The state or ability to see clearly.

Focusing on ourselves is something overlooked because we may be working too much or dedicating our time to our significant other. Yes, working hard is good, but forgetting about ourselves is bad. Focusing on improving our weaknesses and issues helps everyone around us. We also need to focus on our kids and teach them life's lessons of being mature and respectful to adults, teachers, and people of authority.

Are you focused today?

YOUR POWER

Day Eight – 8

Today I will focus on . . .

_____
_____
_____
_____
_____
_____
_____
_____
_____
_____
_____
_____
_____
_____
_____
_____
_____
_____
_____
_____
_____
_____

JOURNAL TO YOUR POWER

What, why, because . . .

YOUR POWER

I

*"one of the most sincere forms
of respect is actually listening
to what another has to say"
...Bryant H McGill*

Listen

To hear someone with focusing of what they are saying; paying attention to someone's words they're speaking to you.

Do you know that we talk too much? We are always trying to get our point across, causing us to miss out on information we need to hear.

Thinking that we are right about a situation does not mean we need to talk others into thinking we are right. Sometimes just being silent is louder than any words we can say.

The Bible tells us to be slow to anger and slow to speak.

Just shhh . . . and listen. It seems so hard yet so easy.

YOUR POWER

Day Nine – 9

Today I will listen to . . .

JOURNAL TO YOUR POWER

Who, why, because . . .

YOUR POWER

FAITH

"time spent in prayer is never wasted"
...Francis Fenelon

Pray

Praying is an act or expression of talking to a higher power, alone or with others. Praying can clear your mind, body, and spirit.

When praying for others, it frees your mind from thinking about your own problems and concerns. Opening your heart to a higher power and giving of yourself; gives you inner peace.

Starting your day with prayer asking for guidance and direction will give you positive energy for the day. Try praying daily. Do it for yourself; you won't be sorry.

YOUR POWER

Day Ten – 10

Today I will pray for or pray about . . .

___

Who, why, because . . .

YOUR POWER

MANY

"don't wait for people to locate you. Rather reach out to people and help bring them to Christ"
...Sunday Adelaja

Reaching Out

We all know someone that is in need. Reaching out with a helping hand is always welcomed by everyone.

Reaching out to our children is often overlooked by our busy lives. Family and friends are in need more than we know! Many people don't mention that they are in need. Many suffer behind closed doors or in humble quietness who are in need of emotional help or for someone to talk to, listen to, cook for, or just sit with.

Reach out and touch someone and make this world a better place.

YOUR POWER

Day Eleven – 11

Today I will reach out to . . .

JOURNAL TO YOUR POWER

Who, why, because . . .

YOUR POWER

EVERYDAY

*"an apology is the super glue of life.
It can repair just about anything"
...Lynn Johnston*

Apologize

To express regret for something that one has done wrong or blamed; to show that you feel badly about any faults caused.

Apologizing is asking for forgiveness of yourself in exchange for a sign of relief that someone has overlooked your faults.

Being able to apologize shows strength and also helps you feel better.

Do yourself a favor and just apologize, please. It makes you the bigger person.

YOUR POWER

Day Twelve – 12

Today I will apologize to . . . for . . .

Who, why, because . . .

YOUR POWER

EVERYONE

"a compliment is verbal sunshine"
...Robert orben

Compliment

A compliment is something that completes, makes perfect, enhances, or improves a situation or person.

A compliment can be a positive adjective to make someone feel good and smile.

Example: you look nice, pretty, younger, thinner.

Try to make a new habit of giving someone a compliment every day. The smile you will receive will make you feel good inside.

Make someone's day. Give them a compliment.
Good job!

YOUR POWER

Day Thirteen – 13

Today I will compliment . . .

_____
_____
_____
_____
_____
_____
_____
_____
_____
_____
_____
_____
_____
_____
_____
_____
_____
_____
_____
_____
_____
_____

JOURNAL TO YOUR POWER

Who, because . . .

YOUR POWER

HAPPINESS

"self-belief and hard work will always earn you success"
...Virut Kohls

Work On

An activity to strengthen or perform something. A physical or mental effort to overcome obstacles to achieve a positive result.

The number one thing we need to do is work on ourselves. It's easy to point fingers at others, of what our friends and family need to work on, but what we need to work on is us! ME!

Pick a thing, emotion or situation, you need to improve about yourself today.
Let's do it . . .

YOUR POWER

Day Fourteen – 14

Today I will work on . . .

JOURNAL TO YOUR POWER

What, why, because . . .

YOUR POWER

GOOD

"yesterday I was clever, so I wanted to change the world. Today I am wise, so I am changing myself"
...Rumi

Change

To change is to make or become different.

Change can be good. Being stuck in the same place physically, emotionally, or spiritually and not knowing is not healthy. Why are we afraid of change?

Take action:

Change the way you think of yourself, people, or a situation. Getting out of your comfort zone helps you make different decisions in your life to cause change for new results.

Go for change, Do change, Be the change. Wow, look at you. (The Game Changer).

YOUR POWER

Day Fifteen – 15

Today I will change my . . .

_____
_____
_____
_____
_____
_____
_____
_____
_____
_____
_____
_____
_____
_____
_____
_____
_____
_____
_____
_____
_____
_____
_____

JOURNAL TO YOUR POWER

What, why, because . . .

YOUR POWER

NEW

"life begins at the end of your comfort zone"
...Neale Donald walsch

Begin

To start, originate, initiate, process, or to come into existence.

Taking a small step to begin anything to move forward in your life is the most positive decision you can make, even if you start something again that you have never finished. Beginning it again is a good place to start.

No more procrastinating. Today I will begin again, and that's okay.

YOUR POWER

Day Sixteen – 16

Today I will begin . . .

JOURNAL TO YOUR POWER

What, why, because . . .

YOUR POWER

NICE

"a hug is like a boomerang you get it back right away"
...Nil Keane

Hug

To squeeze someone tightly in one's arms to show affection; to embrace, cuddle, clutch, or hold someone with positive emotions.

Did you know that there are so many people that are touched-deprived? Did you know that a small gesture of a hug is giving, loving, caring, and soothing to everyone? Most people underestimate the power of a hug. It's called . . . feels good.

A hug lets someone know that they are there for them in their time of need.

A hug to our children helps them learn affection as they get older.

Let's bring it in . . . give me a hug . . .

YOUR POWER

Day Seventeen – 17

Today I will hug . . .

JOURNAL TO YOUR POWER

Who, who, and who? No reason needed.

YOUR POWER

LIFE

"*life is like a movie, write your own ending. Keep believing and keep pretending*"
...Jim Henson

Redo

To do something again or differently.

There's nothing wrong with doing something over. Having the courage to say to yourself, "I need to redo this," is a good thing. Making changes and trying new things helps you learn and grow.

Redoing a class, a project, or your resume invites a new outlook and vision to see things differently.

A do-over is a Redo. Let's make it fun this time. I like it . . .

YOUR POWER

Day Eighteen – 18

Today I will redo . . .

JOURNAL TO YOUR POWER

What, why, because . . .

YOUR POWER

EVERYTHING

"there's always a way, if you are committed"
...Tony Robbins

Commit

To carry out; engage, accomplish, or decide to be all in.

Today is a new day to make a commitment:

Commit to an exercise routine.
Commit to eating healthier.
Commit to being neater.
Commit to smiling more.
Commit to not worrying.
Commit to praying more.
Commit to love yourself in spite of your faults.

Be open to being committed. It's ok, I know you can do it . . .

YOUR POWER

Day Nineteen – 19

Today I will commit to . . .

JOURNAL TO YOUR POWER

What, why, because . . .

YOUR POWER

OVERCOME

"If something is not good enough stop doing it"
...Jonathan Ive

Stop

When an event, action, or process comes to an end.

Let's improve our life and stop pretending that it's easy to stop something. There are many habits that we need to quit.

Stop smoking.
Stop overeating.
Stop being in denial.
Stop lying.
Stop drinking.
Stop driving too fast.
Stop any drug addiction.
Stop missing class.

Stop giving in and stop thinking that you can't stop because you really, really can!

YOUR POWER

Day Twenty – 20

Today I will stop . . .

JOURNAL TO YOUR POWER

What, why, because . . .

YOUR POWER

YOURSELF

"the past cannot be changed the future is yet in your power"
...unknown

Encourage

To give support, confidence, or hope to continue to do something; to help stimulate or develop.

We all need to be encouraged in our lives. Encouragement helps us move to the next level in a positive direction.

Try to support your family, friends, and strangers in their dreams even if you don't believe in them.

One day the shoe may be on the other foot and we will need and want encouragement too.

YOUR POWER

Day Twenty-one – 21

Today I will encourage . . .

_____
_____
_____
_____
_____
_____
_____
_____
_____
_____
_____
_____
_____
_____
_____
_____
_____
_____
_____
_____
_____
_____

Who, why, because . . .

YOUR POWER

INSPIRE

"strive for continuous Improvement, instead of perfection"
...Kim Collins

Improve

To make or become better; to update, enhance, polish, or buildup.

Everyone needs improvement. Let's improve our attitudes, improve our work ethics, improve our listening skills, improve our cooking skills, and improve our outlook of life.

Improving makes us better at anything we want to do.

YOUR POWER

Day Twenty-two – 22

Today I will improve . . .

What, because . . .

YOUR POWER

NOW

"there is no love without forgiveness, and there is no forgiveness Without Love"
...Bryant H McGill

Forgive

To stop feeling angry, resentful, or offensive toward something or someone; to excuse, pardon, or allow.

Did you know that forgiveness is one of the highest powers of the universe?

Forgiving gives you that freedom to move on and let go of any negative situation.

Forgiving makes you the better person and gives you the power.

Here's a secret; forgiving yourself first helps you forgive others easier. Try it.

YOUR POWER

Day Twenty-three – 23

Today I will forgive . . .

_____
_____
_____
_____
_____
_____
_____
_____
_____
_____
_____
_____
_____
_____
_____
_____
_____
_____
_____
_____

JOURNAL TO YOUR POWER

Who, because . . .

YOUR POWER

FREE

"nothing in the universe can stop you from letting go and starting over"
...Guy Finley

Let Go of

To stop holding onto something; to stop thinking about or being angry about the past.

Letting go is hard at times. We hold onto habits, material things, and even people. Letting go of any of the above that is not giving you happiness in your life is the best decision you could ever make.

Let's do the old saying . . .

Let go and let God!

YOUR POWER

Day Twenty-four – 24

Today I will let go of . . .

_____
_____
_____
_____
_____
_____
_____
_____
_____
_____
_____
_____
_____
_____
_____
_____
_____
_____
_____
_____

JOURNAL TO YOUR POWER

What or who, because . . .

YOUR POWER

FINALLY

"love yourself. Forgive yourself. Be true to yourself. How you treat yourself sets the standard for how others will treat you."
...Steve Marabol

Treat Yourself

Treating yourself is acknowledging that you are worthy of everything.

Working overtime that is not appreciated, helping others without a thank you, and staying up all night studying for a big test for school is deserving of a treat.

Sometimes we just have to love ourselves and give ourselves a treat.

Treat yourself. You deserve it.

YOUR POWER

Day Twenty-five – 25

Today I will treat myself to . . .

JOURNAL TO YOUR POWER

What, why, because . . .

YOUR POWER

HEALING

"I believe that laughter is a language of God and that we can all live happily ever laughter"
...Yakovi Smirnoff

Laugh About

Why is life so serious? Guess what? It doesn't have to be.

Laughter improves our health and outlook on life.

Laughing reduces stress, improves your mood, and helps everyone relax.

If something sounds too good to be true, just laugh it off.

Live, love, and laugh.

YOUR POWER

Day Twenty-six – 26

Today I will laugh about . . .

JOURNAL TO YOUR POWER

What, because . . .

YOUR POWER

UNIVERSE

"your success depends mainly upon what you think of yourself and whether you believe in yourself"
...William J H Boetcher

Believe

To strongly feel sure of the truth.
To be convinced that something is going to be or will definitely happen.

Believe in people.
Believe in yourself.
Believe in faith.
Believe in miracles.
Believe in God!

. . . and you will go further in life. Just believe!

YOUR POWER

Day Twenty-seven – 27

Today I will believe in . . .

JOURNAL TO YOUR POWER

What, because . . .

YOUR POWER

PAST

*"let's forget the baggage of the past
and make a new beginning"
...Shehbaz Sharif*

Forget About

To fail to remember.

If we could just stop remembering all the bad in our relationships.

If we could just stop going over and over all the hurtful things people said about us.

If we could stop saying I forgive you but will never forget.

Why can't we just forget about it and move on?

YOUR POWER

Day Twenty-eight – 28

Today I will forget about . . .

___

JOURNAL TO YOUR POWER

What or who, because . . .

YOUR POWER

PRESENT

*"Stand up, face your fears
or they will defeat you"
...LL Cool J*

Stand up For

Standing up for what you believe is the beginning of your success.

Standing up for loved ones and supporting them in a situation shows you are a person of great dignity and honor.

Don't ever let anyone put you down.

Stand up for what you believe in, stand up for what you know, and stand up for you!

YOUR POWER

Day Twenty-nine – 29

Today I will stand up for . . .

JOURNAL TO YOUR POWER

What, because . . .

YOUR POWER

POWERFUL

"*love is the only Force capable of transforming an enemy into a friend*"
...Martin Luther King Jr.

Love

Love is an intense feeling of deep affection. Did you know that love is the number one power you can have within yourself?

Love is needed by everyone.
Love is accepted by everyone.
Love is easy to give.
Love is easy to receive.
Love is powerful.

And,

Love conquers all.

YOUR POWER

Day Thirty – 30

Today I will love . . .

JOURNAL TO YOUR POWER

Who, because . . .

YOUR POWER

Notes

JOURNAL TO YOUR POWER

Notes

Conclusion

From me to you:

Wow! You did it. You looked inside your heart, your thoughts, and your feelings. You opened up all your hidden secrets stored in your spirit to verbalize your healing.

"*Go!Do!Be!*"
    Trish Moore

Go back and reread your journal and be empowered with your own words.

This book is now: YOUR POWER JOURNAL

JOURNAL TO YOUR POWER

Please pick up another copy of this book for a friend, family members, or yourself again. This is a great book for your teenager to empower them; they can create their own book club using this journal to bond with their friends to learn and grow from each other . . .

Thank you for choosing this book.

I appreciate YOU.

About the Author

Patricia Moore, aka "*Miss Trish*", is a licensed massage therapist of over 18 years who has studied Life Coaching, Personal Training, Nutrition, and EFT, an emotional tapping stress relieving technique, an entrepreneur, and now author.

Miss Trish is a single parent and an only child raised by her mother. After her father passed away when she was five-years-old, her mother encouraged her to be independent and to always help anyone in need. Remembering what her mother taught her, Miss Trish took in one of her daughter's high school girlfriends who was in a bad living environment to live with them for one school year.

Miss Trish's passion is to be a blessing to people who come into her life whether it's through massage, listening, nutritional advice, or coaching in a positive direction of empowerment.

CPSIA information can be obtained
at www.ICGtesting.com
Printed in the USA
LVHW020047140420
653367LV00003B/638